CHARLES LEDERER

Presents

EDWIN LESTER'S

Production of

# KISMET

A Musical Arabian Night

shown

Music and Lyrics

ROBERT WRIGHT and GEORGE FORREST
(Based on themes of Alexander Borodin)

*Book by*

CHARLES LEDERER and LUTHER DAVIS
(Based on the play by Edward Knoblock)

Orchestral and Choral Arrangements by ARTHUR KAY
Production Directed by ALBERT MARRE
Dances and Musical Numbers Staged by JACK COLE
Settings and Costumes Designed by LEMUEL AYERS
Lighting by PEGGY CLARK
Musical Direction by LOUIS ADRIAN

## VOCAL SCORE
(Edited by Louis C. Singer)

HAL•LEONARD®
CORPORATION
7777 W. BLUEMOUND RD. P.O. BOX 13819 MILWAUKEE, WI 53213

# NOTICE

Purchase of this vocal score does not entitle the purchaser to perform the work in public. All rights including public performances for profit are reserved to the authors. For information regarding performances of the work write to:

MUSIC THEATRE INTERNATIONAL
545 8th Avenue, New York, NY 10018
(212) 868-66668

## COMPOSERS' NOTE:

The following cast list is preserved solely for historical accuracy. In the *Authorized Revised Version* of the script some characters have been deleted, some added, some have had their titles altered. In this authorized revised version of the Piano-Vocal Score, on all pages other than this 1953 cast list, the characters' names, titles, dialog and musical cues will conform to the *Authorized Revised Version* of the script.

The Edwin Lester production of KISMET was first presented by Charles Lederer at the Ziegfeld Theatre, New York City, on December 3, 1953, with the following cast:

| | |
|---|---|
| IMAM OF THE MOSQUE | RICHARD ONETO |
| MUEZZINS | GERALD CARDONI<br>KIRBY SMITH<br>RALPH STRANE<br>LOUIS POLACEK |
| DOORMAN | JACK MEI LING |
| FIRST BEGGAR | EARLE MACVEIGH |
| SECOND BEGGAR | ROBERT LAMONT |
| THIRD BEGGAR | RODOLFO SILVA |
| DERVISHES | JACK DODDS<br>MARC WILDER |
| OMAR KHAYYAM | PHILIP COOLIDGE |
| A PUBLIC POET, LATER CALLED HAJJ | ALFRED DRAKE |
| MARSINAH, HIS DAUGHTER | DORETTA MORROW |
| A MERCHANT | KIRBY SMITH |
| HASSAN-BEN | HAL HACKETT |
| JAWAN | TRUMAN GAIGE |
| STREET DANCER | FLORENCE LESSING |
| AKBAR | JACK DODDS |
| ASSIZ | MARC WILDER |
| THE BANGLE MAN | RICHARD ONETO |
| CHIEF POLICEMAN | TOM CHARLESWORTH |
| SECOND POLICEMAN | HAL HACKETT |
| THE WAZIR OF POLICE | HENRY CALVIN |
| WAZIR'S GUARDS | STEVEN FERRY<br>STEVE REEVES |
| LALUME | JOAN DIENER |
| ATTENDANTS | MARIO LAMM<br>JOHN WEIDERMANN |
| THE PRINCESSES OF ABABU | PATRICIA DUNN<br>BONNIE EVANS<br>REIKO SATO |
| THE CALIPH | RICHARD KILEY |
| SLAVE GIRLS | CAROL OHMART<br>JOYCE PALMER<br>SANDRA STAHL<br>LILA JACKSON |
| A PEDDLER | EARLE MACVEIGH |
| A SERVANT | RICHARD VINE |
| PRINCESS ZUBBEDIYA OF DAMASCUS | FLORENCE LESSING |
| AYAH TO ZUBBEDIYA | LUCY ANDONIAN |
| PRINCESS SAMAHRIS OF BANGALORE | BEATRICE KRAFT |
| AYAH TO SAMAHRIS | THELMA DARE |
| STREET WOMEN | JO ANN O'CONNELL<br>LYNNE STUART |
| PROSECUTOR | EARLE MACVEIGH |
| THE WIDOW YUSSEF | BARBARA SLATE |
| DIWAN DANCERS | NEILE ADAMS<br>JACK DODDS<br>MARC WILDER |

SINGERS: Gerald Cardoni, Robert Lamont, Richard Oneto, Louis Polacek, Kirby Smith, Ralph Strane, Richard Vine, George Yarick.
Anita Coulter, Thelma Dare, Lila Jackson, Jo Ann O'Connell, Barbara Slate, Sandra Stahl, Lynne Stuart, Erica Twiford.

DANCERS: Neile Adams, Patricia Dale, Devra Kline, Ania Romaine, Vida Ann Solomon, Roberta Stevenson.

# SCENES

ONE DAY IN BAGHDAD,
CAPITAL OF THE ABBASID
CALIPHATE, IN A.D. 1071

## ACT ONE

(From Dawn to Dusk)

## ACT TWO

(From Dusk to Dawn)

# TABLE OF CONTENTS

## ACT ONE

## ACT TWO

# OVERTURE
### and
# SANDS OF TIME
(Opening - Act I)

No. 1

By ROBERT WRIGHT
and GEORGE FORREST

Moderato

"BAUBLES, BANGLES AND BEADS"
Andante con moto

"NOT SINCE NINEVEH"
Bright

"STRANGER IN PARADISE"
Espressivo con moto

"SANDS OF TIME"
Andante cantabile, but with movement
IMAM *(walking slowly toward the mosque)*

Prin-ces come, Prin-ces go, _____ An ho-ur of pomp and show _____

_____ they know; Prin-ces come, _____ And o-ver the sands, And o-ver the

sands of time, _____ They go! _____

Wise men come, Ev-er prom-is-ing _____ The rid-dle of life to know;

Wise men come, Ah, but o-ver the sands, The si-lent sands of time, _____

soul_____ shriv - els,____ shriv - els!_____ Pray, ____ pray!

**1st BEGGAR:**
Every morning that same horrible noise!

What an hour to start working!
Sometimes I wish I wasn't a beggar!

*(To 2nd Beggar)*
Get up! Get up! Start suffering!
*(Cue:) (Sound of people approaching)*
Customers! Hurry - - - - -

**Freely** *(follow dialogue)*
Fl.
*p*
Cl.

*(Beggars cry for alms as morning worshippers enter and cross into mosque.)*

*(OMAR KHAYYAM enters)*

*Cue to cut off*

OMAR: *(To whirling dervish beggar)*
Oh, stop it!

**Allegro agitato** *(repeat ad lib.)*
Fl ,Cl.
*mf*
Strgs. R.H.

*Warning:* THE POET: Too early to eat,
                   Too early to . . . bed,
*Cue:* THE POET: But never, oh never
                 Too early to sing!

(Dialogue continues.)

MARSINAH: A sale, father? A sale? Breakfast?
(entering)

THE POET: Noble gentlemen whose eyes have been turned toward heaven—a rhyme to bring them back to earth?

Cue:
Choose your topic:    Weddings?
(Ad lib.)

*Cue:* **THE POET:** I sat down, feeling desolated, Bowed my head and crossed my knees ___
Is fortune really predicated upon such tiny turns as these?

*(Continuing, over music)* Then Fate's a thing without a head, A puzzle never understood,
And man proceeds where he is led, unguaranteed of bad or good.

To weave the e-vil and good In one de - sign! _____ And

so, _____ my Des-ti - ny, _____ I look at you _____ and can-not see _____ Is it

*poco a poco accel.*

**Bright**

good, is it ill? Am I blessed, am I cursed? Is it hon - ey on my tongue or

brine? _____ What fate, _____ what

*mp*

Vls.

*(THE POET runs to the steps of the*

fate _____ is mine? _____

W. W.

*mp* Brass

Cl., Ob.

*cresc.*

blessed, am I cursed? Is it hon-ey on my tongue or brine?_____

add Hns.

_____ What fate, _____ what fate _____ is m...

Vls., W.W.

Dramatic
Brass

HASSAN-BEN:
You on the steps—are you
the beggar called Hajj?

*(Dialogue continues)*
*Cue:* **THE POET:**
*Far and wide the
name of Hajj is....*

Brass

*Cue:*
**THE POET: Permit me to correct myself, my name
is not Hajj....**

simile

*Cue:*
**THE POET: Who are you? What do you want? I am not Hajj - -!
You are making a terrible, terrible, terrible mistake!**

*Cue:*
**THE POET: WHERE? ARE? MY? FIGS?**

*Segue
as one.*

# THE HAND OF FATE
### (Change of Scene)

*Cue:* (*Segue from No. 3*)

# FATE - REPRISE

*Warning:* **THE POET:** And now leave me to my prayers. *(He starts to kneel.)* Excuse me, which way *is* Mecca?

*Cue: The brigands point, THE POET kneels.*

# No.6        BAZAAR OF THE CARAVANS

*Cue: (Segue from No. 5)*

32

*Warning:* **WAZIR:**...... See how well they laugh without teeth!
         **POLICEMAN:** It shall be done, Oh Wazir.
         **1st GUARD:** *(Off stage)* Wife of Wives to the Wazir!
*Cue:*      **2nd GUARD:** *(On stage)* Wife of Wives to the Wazir! Persons of ordinary rank, clear the Bazaar!

## No. 8        ABABU DANCE I
### (Drum Solo)

*Warning:* **WAZIR:** .... Are these Ababus attractive?
*Cue:* **LALUME:**..... Assume your gentlest manner...the Princesses are already homesick...and as shy as a little herd of deer.
         Exalted Wazir, I present their Royal Highnesses, the Princesses of Ababu!

# NOT SINCE NINEVEH

*Warning: (Townspeople enter and scramble for coins )*
*Cue:* **LALUME:** Our city is the world's gayest playground!
There's been nothing like it for a thousand years!

prin - ces more _____ au - to - crat - ic here, _____ Our

Vls.,W.W.

beg - gars more dis - tinct - ly ar - o - mat - ic here! _____

Vls.,W.W.

mf

Where could you Ev - er pur - sue Your life _____

With the zeal _____ we feel here? Not since Bab-y-lon

read that writ-ing, Not since Jer-i - cho heard that trum-pet, Not since Neb-u-chad-nez-zar's hanging

Segue
on
Applause

*(Wazir and Lalume beckon townspeople to join them downstage in the "sales pitch")*
Bright *(but with strong bounce.)*

No. 11

# EXIT AFTER NINEVEH
## and
## STOLEN ORANGES

*Cue: (Wazir signals to Macho Males, who take Princesses*
*pick-a-back to Wazir's palace)*

*Broadly*          *(Princesses, Lalume, Wazir exit)*

Piano

*(Merchants and Vendors resume their cries. [from No. 6]) (Marsinah runs on, chased by orange merchant)*

Agitato

*(Dialogue)*

No. 12

# SLAVE MERCHANT'S CRY

*Cue: . . . things he invents in his own head?*
SLAVE MERCHANT: *(With force, hawking his wares)*

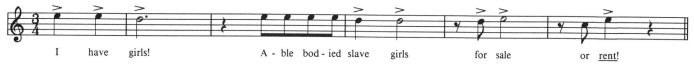

I have girls!     A - ble bod - ied slave girls    for sale    or rent!

# No.13  BAUBLES, BANGLES AND BEADS

*Warning:* **THE POET:** Well, you should have maids and attendants now....
*Cue:* **THE POET:** I'll get three or four. <u>N</u>o sense being shorthanded!

Rhythmically, not legato; sung with urgent attack

Moderato; sung rhythmically, with humorous emphasis

PEARL MERCHANT:
Think up-on the Mac-e - do - ni-an oys-ter Hav-ing in-di-ges-tion in his
(dye)

P.M.
wa - ter-y clois - ter So that Mar-si-nah could have a pearl, _____ A

Meno mosso                    Allegretto moderato
                              MARSINAH:
P.M.
pearl,        a pearl!              Bau - bles,        ban - gles,
                                    (Baw)
BANGLE MAN:
Bau-bles,        ban-gles        and        beads!

M.
Hear how they jing, jing-a - ling - a, Bau - bles, ban - gles,

*(Marsinah and girls exit to "dressing" booth)*

*(Dialogue - Omar and Caliph.)*

*Warning:* OMAR: If you fall in love in Bagdad, get thee to Damascus.
And if you fall in love in Damascus, get thee to Bagdad.

*Cue:* OMAR: Before I was known as the Tentmaker, I was called <u>Omar the Traveller</u>. *(gestures of speedy travel back and forth)*

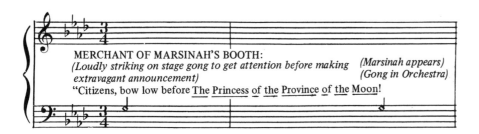

MERCHANT OF MARSINAH'S BOOTH:
*(Loudly striking on stage gong to get attention before making    (Marsinah appears)*
*extravagant announcement)    (Gong in Orchestra)*
"Citizens, bow low before <u>The Princess of the Province of the Moon</u>!

No. 14        PARADISE GARDEN

# No. 15        STRANGER IN PARADISE

*Warning:* CALIPH: I know. Most things <u>I</u> love don't exist. About . . . about your daughter's father. You say he's a gardener?
*Cue:* <u>I garden, too.</u>

**C.** But o - pen your an-gel's arms ____ To the stran-ger in Pa - a - dise

Vls.

Celeste
Strgs.

*(Omar enters, unseen by Marsinah. He gestures impatiently)*

**C.** And tell him that he need be ____ A stran-ger no more.

*rall.*

W.W.

Hp. Solo

*rall.*

*fp*

MARSINAH: Uhh- - - - -What kind of flowers should I plant along the fence?

A tempo    Celeste

Vl.I Solo

*pp*    Strgs

*(Omar signals)* CALIPH: I must go. Forgive me. Please- -would you meet me here this evening?

Fl. Solo

CALIPH: At moon-rise? Here in the garden?    MARSINAH: At moonrise?    CALIPH: Please.

## No. 16     THE POET AND THE SLAVE GIRLS

THE POET: Would you like to rest a while, ladies?
*(Dialogue continues.)*

## No. 17     THE POET'S ARREST

*Warning:* THE POET: Uhh, Allah, Buddha, and Confucius, etc.
*Cue:* *(Policeman's jerk on chain knocks the Poet off his feet.)*

*Direct segue to No. 18*
*"The Wazir's Palace"*

**No. 18**

# THE WAZIR'S PALACE

Cue: *(direct segue from No. 17)*

**No. 19**

# THE WAZIR'S COUNCIL

*Warning:* WAZIR: I always feel better when I sentence people.
*Cue:* CHIEF POLICEMAN: The evening Court of Justice convenes!

# No. 20 GESTICULATE

*Warning:* **THE POET:** Hold! For that simple sentence you needed your <u>hand</u>...
      **LALUME:** Oh let him. I love being convinced.
*Cue:* (*Wazir gestures his permission.*)

**P:** tail___ Like a spout-less whale,___ Like an el-e-phant,

**W:** Drag this de-bris out the door! A bore! A bore!___ So

**W.C.** *(Guards lift the Poet and start to exit.)* Drag this de-bris out the door! Drag this de-bris out the door!

Drag this de-bris out the door!

Vls., Cls., Hns. *cresc.*

LALUME: *(All turn sharply to Lalume.)*

Hold!_____ I'd like to hear a lit-tle

**P.** sunk If you cut off his trunk!

**W.** do as I or-dered be-fore!

**W.C.** door!___

Freely, as a cadenza

# THE CALIPH'S NEWS
(Three Fanfares)

*Warning:* **WAZIR:** Wait! Wait!
*Cue:* What became of that curse?

FANFARE I

Maestoso *(con moto)*

Piano

*ff* Brass

*Cue:* **HERALD:** Bow low! The Highest of the High!

FANFARE II

Maestoso *(con moto)*

*ff*

*Cue:* **CALIPH:** May every citizen share his Caliph's happiness!

FANFARE III

**WAZIR:** Ruined! etc.

Maestoso *(con moto)*

*ff*

*f*

## No. 22    THE WEDDING PARTY

V O I C E S

O. S.

*Cue:* ...Not the Princesses, of course. *(Loudly, with spirit, accompanied by on stage cymbals, drums, etc.*

*etc. as needed*

Play on the cym - bal, the tim - bal, the ly - re, play with ap - pro - pri - ate pas - sion, fash - ion...

## No. 23    FATE-FINALE ACT I

*Note: The keys of the 2 Solo Harem Girl phrases below are not important, only the registers. They take their cues from dialogue on stage, not from Conductor.*

*Cue:* **THE POET:** Poor humans we, suspended between abyss and infinity,...

Lento

**SOLO HAREM GIRL:** *(as the Poet continues)*

*p* Ah!

*(She repeats ad lib. until cue: "It is thy choice!")*

*Cue:* **THE POET:** Below and above and in the swirling darkness.

**2nd SOLO HAREM GIRL:** *(as the Poet continues)*

Moderato

*mf* Ah!

*(She repeats ad lib. until cue: "It is thy choice!")*

*Warning -* **THE POET:** Remove our Caliph's love for this woman. Or remove the woman from our Caliph ___

*Cue:* It is thy choice!

Allegro

*mf*

**HAREM GIRL:**

*(Scream)*

**LALUME and HAREM GIRLS:**

*mf*

Sha - bash! Sha - bash!

*mf*

**TIMPANI**

(Lalume points straight up, indicating Poet's ascension)

(Play as curtain hits floor.)

(Hold as curtain falls)

"STRANGER IN PARADISE"

"BAUBLES, BANGLES AND BEADS"
Andante con moto

"NOT SINCE NINEVEH"

# NIGHT OF MY NIGHTS

### No. 25

(Opening - Act II)

*(Composers Note: This instrumental introductory music can be effective as either a nuptial procession, or a brief oriental bridal dance.)*

*Cue:* OMAR: . . .No one in your family ever married
in this district before.
*(Caliph, gesturing to Royal Musicians onstage)*

**Moderato** *(with a lilt)*

CALIPH:

Play on the cym-bal, the tim-bal, the ly - re, Play with ap -

pro-pri-ate pas-sion; fash-ion Songs of de - light and de -

li - cious de - sire— For the night of my nights!

Come where the

so well be - lov - ed is wait-ing, Where the

*Cue: (Segue from No. 25)*

*(Marsinah enters the garden to keep her "Moonrise Rendezvous")*

## No. 27 BAUBLES, BANGLES AND BEADS-REPRISE

*Warning:* OMAR: What a simple, unaffected girl she must be.
*Cue:* (*Caliph signals offstage lute player, and sings toward the house*)

# NIGHT OF MY NIGHTS - REPRISE

*Warning:* OMAR: It is only those who love well whom love can hurt.
*Cue: (Unthinking, Omar gives signal; he slams shut the lid of jewel box)*

**Very Lively**
ENTOURAGE: *(Running on stage) (Loudly, joyously)*

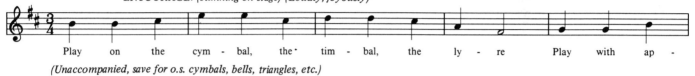

Play on the cym - bal, the tim - bal, the ly - re Play with ap -

*(Unaccompanied, save for o.s. cymbals, bells, triangles, etc.)*

pro - pri - ate pas - sion, fash - ion Songs of de - light and de -

li - cious de - si - re For the night of my Ni - -

*(During above, Omar runs frantically among the singers.)*

OMAR: No, No! It's a mistake! Quiet! Stop!
*(Singing comes to a ragged halt)*

**No. 29**

# THE EMPTY LITTER
### and
# THE WAZIR'S SPIES

*Warning:* OMAR: . . . Sing <u>loudly</u> so that no one will know that there <u>is</u> no bride!
*Cue:* CALIPH: . . . <u>Forgive me if I do not join you.</u>

Moderato, vigorously
Hand Cym.
ENTOURAGE: *(exiting)*

Play on the cym - bal, the tim - bal, the ly - re,

Strgs., W. W.

Piano

Hns., Bn.

Play with ap - pro - pri - ate pas - sion; fash - ion Songs of de -

*(exiting)*

light and de - li - cious de - sire,— For the night of my

*(Alone and rueful, his heart clearly broken)*
CALIPH:
*(Caliph exits, still singing softly)*

nights! _____ 'Tis the night of my nights!
Slower
Tempo I°
*Ad lib.*
Cue: *(Lights <u>entirly out</u>.)*

**No. 30**                    WAS I WAZIR ?

*Warning:* LALUME: If I told you, you'd just be - - - angry.
*Cue:* WAZIR: . . Subtlety, always subtlety. Anyone can be violent or crude, but subtlety has put me where I am!

# THE POETS MEET

*Cue: Wazir exits.*
*(With music, two female attendants enter,*
*play pantomime with The Poet, pedestal*
*and looking-glass. Omar enters, sees The*
*Poet primping in mirror, and speaks.*
*Music stops.)*

## No. 32        THE OLIVE TREE

*Warning:* OMAR: . . . Here's a poem with sense and quickness, etc.
*Cue:* THE POET: Omar, my friend, there's always something to be learned . . . <u>even</u> from <u>fools</u>.

A fool_____ sat be - neath an ol - ive tree_____ And a

P.
wondrous thought had he, So he rose and he told it to the
sky. And where was I? Behind the tree. I over-heard His rever-
rit.
Lively
Fl. Ob.
ie:
p Vls.
Cello, Bass
Cl.
"Why be content with an
olive When you could have the tree?
Vls.Cls.
Why be content to be nothing When there's nothing you

124

For I walked — with my eye up-on a star! If you have

*poco rall.*
heard And do not heed, There is a word For what you

*a tempo*    *rit.*
are, And oh, my friend, The word is

Lively
"fool!"

*poco rit.*

Segue on Applause

No. 33

# RAHADLAKUM
(Koom)

*Warning: (End of No. 32)*
*Cue: (Curtain starts up during blackout.)*

Moderately slow but very rhythmic *(in 2)*
*(The Harem Girls are entertaining The Poet.)*

LALUME: Dear Hajj, our new Emir. My exalted husband has instructed me to make you happy - - delight you - -

LALUME: *(spoken)*
"Feed you sweetmeats"

La-dies___ shall we be-gin ser-vice?

L. hand - maid-en hath what he lack-eth, And what doth he

L. lack?

THE POET: (As before)
Ra - ha - had - la - kum! 'Tis

Mandolin attach. off
Trpts., Trbs.

P. sweet with the meat of the li-chi nut Com-bined with the kum-quat

Bells

P. rind, The kind of con-fec-tion To drive a man out of His

Ob.

P. He turn-eth his face,_____ His pre-vi-ous place in her em-brace He doth re-

LALUME:
And love is in bloom_____ The while they con-

P. sume!_____ And love is in bloom_____ The while they con-

L. sume_____ Ra ha_____ ha_____

P. sume_____ Ra-ha_____ Ra-ha_____ ha_____ ha_____

AYAH:
Ra-ha_____ ha_____ ha_____

Brass

**Bright**

No. 34     AND THIS IS MY BELOVED

*Cue:* CALIPH: . . . notify the entire force of the following assignment. They must find the young lady, the girl I told you I am determined to marry. Are you ready to receive details? *(Music begins)*

CALIPH: I first saw her this noontime in the Bazaar of the Caravans. She was alone, purchasing clothing. *(over music)*

146

**No. 35**　　　　　　　　　THE CALIPH'S DIWAN

*Warning:* WAZIR: . . . I will vist her tonight.
*Cue:* WAZIR: . . . a very entertaining bridal night - - for a change! *(Blackout)*

**No. 36**           ZUBBEDIYA

*Warning:* OMAR: Oh Prince of True Believers, the first of the maidens. . . .
*Cue:* OMAR: . . . agile as the mongoose! Zubbediya of Zanzibar!

No. 37

# SAMAHRIS' DANCE

# No. 38   ABABU DANCE II

*Warning: (End of No. 37)*
*Cue:* OMAR: . . . that third of you which she can serve best. The Princesses of Ababu!

## Drum Solo

**Not too fast**

No. 39          FROM THE RUBAIYAT

*Warning:* CALIPH: ... The cadence to prove the futility of love?
*Cue:* OMAR: ... No one could prove it more conclusively. Not even Euclid.

Cue: WAZIR: ... Look at him, descendant of Mohammed, outwitted by an ordinary mortal! It just goes to prove it doesn't sharpen a man's mind.

THE POET: Behold! etc.

No. 40          THE WAZIR IS DEAD

*Warning:* THE POET: A bargain, great Caliph! Name me his sentence first!
         CALIPH: I would order his death without delay and without mercy!
*Cue:* THE POET: I thank you for your verdict! It has been carried out!

*Warning:* THE POET: Condemn him to lighten her sorrows....
*Cue:* LALUME: You have just sentenced yourself to a <u>lifetime</u> <u>of</u> <u>hard</u> <u>labor</u>! *(she exits)*

THE POET: And finally, oh Prince of True Believers, take from Hajj his greatest treasure, his daughter
Marsinah. Take her away forever by marrying her to the end of her days.

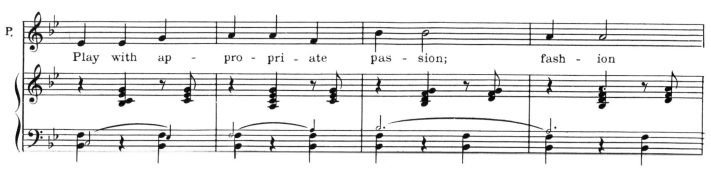

P. For the night of their nights! _____

R.H.

CALIPH:
Come where the so well be - lov - ed is wait - ing....

simile

MARSINAH:
Where the rose and the jas - mine min - gle...

Vl.I.

M. Fl., Ob.
While I tell him the moon is for mat - ing

CALIPH:
While I tell her the moon is for mat - ing

Vls.

162

*(Caliph starts to lead Marsinah upstage. Omar stays behind)*